Economics in Action

What is Insurance?

Baron Bedesky

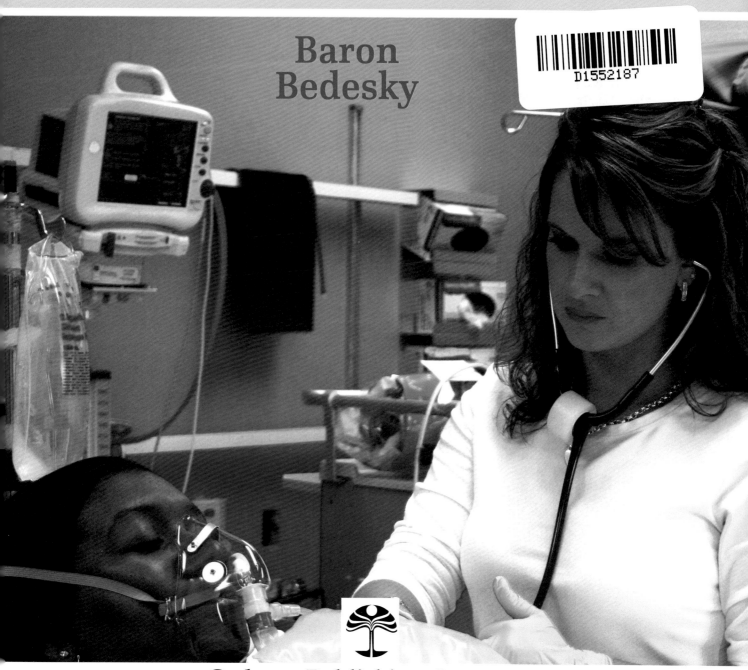

D1552187

Crabtree Publishing Company
www.crabtreebooks.com

Crabtree Publishing Company

www.crabtreebooks.com

Author: Baron Bedesky
Publishing plan research and development:
  Sean Charlebois, Reagan Miller
  Crabtree Publishing Company
Coordinating editor: Chester Fisher
Series editor: Gare Thompson Associates
Editor: Molly Aloian
Proofreader: Crystal Sikkens
Editorial director: Kathy Middleton
Production coordinator: Margaret Salter
Prepress technician: Margaret Salter
Project manager: Kumar Kunal (Q2AMEDIA)
Art direction: Harleen Mehta (Q2AMEDIA)
Cover design: Shruti Aggarwal (Q2AMEDIA)
Design: Shruti Aggarwal (Q2AMEDIA)
Photo research: Ekta Sharma (Q2AMEDIA)

Photographs:
American Honda Motor Co, Inc: p. 27 (bottom)
AP Photo: Vincent Yu: p. 18
Corbis: p. 23; Brooks Kraft: p. 5; Gianni Dagli Orti: p. 9 (bottom);
  Lloyd Cluff: p. 14
Istockphoto: Dave Logan: p. 7; Michel de Nijs: p. 11; Kirby
  Hamilton: p. 21; Gene Chutka: p. 24; James Boulette: p. 29
Masterfile: p. 20
Photolibrary: p. 26; Roy Morsch: p. 9 (top); Hoberman Collection: p.
  12; Keith Levit Photography: p. 17; Superstock: p. 19; Hirb: p. 22;
  Javier Larrea: cover
Q2AMedia Art Bank: p. 8
Reuters: Philippe Wojazer: p. 28
Shutterstock: Alex Neauville: cover, p. 4; Kitti: p. 6; Sonya Etchison:
  p. 10; Anyka: p. 13; Yancy: p. 15; Andrew Gentry: title page, p. 16;
  Curt Ziegler: p. 25; Alexander Raths: p. 27 (top)

Library and Archives Canada Cataloguing in Publication

Bedesky, Baron
    What is insurance? / Baron Bedesky.

(Economics in action)
Includes index.
ISBN 978-0-7787-4444-3 (bound).--ISBN 978-0-7787-4455-9 (pbk.)

1. Insurance--Juvenile literature. I. Title.
II. Series: Economics in action (St. Catherines, Ont.)

HG8052.5.B43 2010   j368   C2009-906269-0

Library of Congress Cataloging-in-Publication Data

Bedesky, Baron.
    What is insurance? / Baron Bedesky.
        p. cm. -- (Economics in action)
Includes index.
ISBN 978-0-7787-4455-9 (pbk. : alk. paper) -- ISBN 978-0-7787-4444-3
(reinforced library binding : alk. paper)
1. Insurance--Juvenile literature. I. Title. II. Series.

HG8052.5.B43 2010
368--dc22

                                        2009042775

Crabtree Publishing Company

www.crabtreebooks.com   1-800-387-7650

Printed in the USA/122009/BG20091103

Published in Canada
Crabtree Publishing
616 Welland Ave.
St. Catharines, ON
L2M 5V6

Published in the United States
Crabtree Publishing
PMB 59051
350 Fifth Avenue, 59th Floor
New York, New York 10118

Published in the United Kingdom
Crabtree Publishing
Maritime House
Basin Road North, Hove
BN41 1WR

Published in Australia
Crabtree Publishing
386 Mt. Alexander Rd.
Ascot Vale (Melbourne)
VIC 3032

Contents

Disaster Strikes

Disasters can hit at anytime. Fires can strike during hot summers. Floods can happen after heavy rainstorms. Earthquakes can suddenly turn cities into rubble. Hurricanes can destroy coastal cities.

On August 29, 2005, Hurricane Katrina struck New Orleans, Louisiana. The rain and fierce winds caused massive destruction throughout the city. Much of New Orleans lies below sea level. In the past, a series of **levees** had protected the area from flooding. But this time those levees failed in more than 50 different locations. The resulting damage was devastating.

Water flooded more than 80 percent of the city and remained in many areas for weeks after the storm hit. More than 1,800 people lost their lives. More than one million people were forced to leave their homes and move to other communities. **Damages** were estimated at $90 billion, making it the most expensive disaster in the history of the United States.

▼ Hurricane Katrina destroyed about 275,000 homes.

New Orleans had to rebuild its levees.

Saved by Insurance

Many people wanted to return and rebuild their homes after the flood waters were drained. Others planned to build new homes in different communities. Luckily, many of these people had **insurance**. Without insurance, very few could have afforded the cost of rebuilding. Their insurance **policy** paid their **claims**. Their claims were for the loss of their homes and possessions, such as furniture, appliances, and automobiles. They received money for the claims so they could replace their homes and possessions.

Insurance did not cover the cost of all the destruction. Most homes and businesses had **coverage** for damage from "wind and driving rain" because of the storm. However, most insurance policies did not cover damage from flooding. Residents who had no flood coverage received very little or no insurance money even though their homes were ruined and they had lost everything. Some businesses and residents did have flood insurance. The United States government had set up the National Flood Insurance Program in 1968. This program assisted private insurance companies in paying claims for flood damage. By May 2006, approximately 162,000 claims from Hurricane Katrina were paid. Insurance helped the people of New Orleans begin rebuilding the city.

Point of Information

Insurance companies paid more than $43 billion in damages resulting from Hurricane Katrina. Approximately 1.75 million claims were made. The companies could afford to make these payments, mostly because they made record **profits** during a three-year period from 2004 to 2006.

What is Insurance?

Insurance is a way of protecting yourself and your belongings from the problems of everyday life. Insurance helps people through hard times. People need insurance to keep them safe.

Accidents can happen. You might get sick. Your house might be robbed or damaged by fire or a natural disaster. You could lose your job. Without insurance, these problems may cost your life savings or force you to sell everything you own.

Insurance provides the money you need to cover the cost of unexpected problems—money you might not otherwise have. You receive the money when you file a claim, or request for payment. Insurance can pay for many different things. It can pay for lost or stolen goods. It can provide money for homes lost in a fire or hurricane so the owners can rebuild or restore their homes. Insurance will also pay to repair a car damaged in an accident. Insurance helps pay for healthcare and provide for one's family in case of death or injury. Even if you lose your job, insurance can help pay your bills until you find a new job. People feel more secure when they have insurance to pay for unexpected expenses.

▲ People have car insurance to protect them in case of an accident.

How Does It Work?

Insurance is a service offered by providers to nearly everyone. People and businesses purchase insurance by paying **premiums**, or fees, to an insurance company.

▲ Home insurance pays for damages to houses caused by fires.

Overhead and Profits

With few exceptions, insurance companies collect more dollars in premiums than they pay in claims. What do insurance companies do with this extra money? Well, insurance companies have many expenses related to running their business. They need office space. They need workers. They also need equipment, such as computers, copiers, and phones. Most insurance companies advertise their services to attract customers. All these costs are called overhead. The premiums that people pay for their insurance help pay for these costs. After paying overhead, any remaining money is profit for the insurance company.

Economics and YOU

Think of insurance simply as a way of protecting yourself. If you were to take vitamin C daily, you would minimize the **risk** of catching a cold. If you pay insurance regularly, you're protecting yourself against the risk of not being able to take care of yourself in an emergency.

Making Money

Companies have to make a profit to stay in business. They need to make money so they can pay the claims made by their clients, pay their overhead, and **invest** in their future business.

Insurance companies make a profit in two different ways. They benefit by collecting more in premiums than they pay in overhead and claims. They also make additional profits by investing the money they collect in premiums. Money can be invested in the stock market, for example, where the value of the investment can grow. (Of course, money invested in the stock market can also lose value.) Their investments help the insurance companies generate money if they should have to pay claims.

How Much to Charge?

Insurance companies have a challenging decision to make when they determine what to charge in premiums. If they don't charge enough, the company will not make a profit. If they charge too much, their premiums will be higher than those of other insurance companies. Insurance companies are in competition with one another. They worry that people will shop around and decide to buy their insurance from the company that offers the lowest premiums.

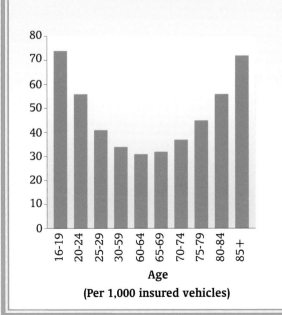

Point of Information

Number of people killed in car accidents in the United States in 2008 by age:

Age

(Per 1,000 insured vehicles)

▲ Elderly drivers pay more for their auto insurance.

Insurance companies conduct research to determine how much to charge people with different profiles. For example, studies show that young automobile drivers have more accidents than drivers in their 40s and 50s. As a result, young drivers pay higher insurance premiums. Elderly people also have more accidents than other age groups so they pay higher insurance premiums, too.

Other factors that affect automobile insurance premiums include driver education for young people, where the driver lives, and how many accidents a driver has had. A driver who lives in a city and has had several fender benders will probably be paying a higher premium than the occasional driver who lives deep in the country. Teens who have taken driver education courses pay less for car insurance than teens who have not taken these courses. Of course, the best way to pay less for your insurance is not to have an accident. Good drivers pay less so be careful!

Point of Information

King Hammurabi of Babylon introduced the first insurance in about 1750 BC. During his rule, sea trade grew dramatically. Theft and loss during shipping became a big problem. Hammurabi decreed that the state would pay back cargo shippers in case of loss or theft during transport.

Many Kinds of Insurance

People protect themselves from unexpected costs by purchasing different types of insurance. Most of us need more than one kind of insurance to keep safe.

Insurance Needs

Why do we need different kinds of insurance? We face many types of risk nearly every day. Bad weather can destroy our property. We can be hurt in an accident or become ill. Many people lose their jobs when their employer must reduce costs. All of us grow old, and many of us need assistance after we can no longer work. Insurance helps people facing all of these problems. Different kinds of insurance protect us from these risks.

▼ There is health insurance for pets.

Individual Insurance		
Type of Insurance	What it covers	When you need it
Property Insurance	Automobiles, homes, furniture, appliances, etc. in homes; lawsuits	When your home is destroyed or damaged; when your car or possessions are damaged or stolen; when a visitor is injured on your property
Life Insurance	Person's life and loss of employment income	When a family member dies, especially if that person's income is supporting the family
Health Insurance	Doctor visits, hospital stays, diagnostic tests, physiotherapy, medicine, dental	When you or other family members get sick or become disabled
Government Benefits	Health care and pensions for elderly, poor, and veterans; unemployment	When you can't provide for yourself
Automobile Insurance	Cost of repair or replacement of cars, trucks, and other vehicles.	When your vehicle has been damaged in an accident and requires costly repairs or replacement.

These are the most popular kinds of insurance. However, we can buy insurance for many other less well-known reasons. For example, farmers can buy crop insurance in case bad weather ruins their harvest. People buy insurance for their pets in case they get sick or hurt and require expensive treatment. Professional singers can even insure their voices.

◀ Farmers insure their crops against bad weather.

Point of Information

Actress America Ferrera, star of the television show *Ugly Betty*, insured her smile for $10 million. The policy is part of a charitable effort providing dental care for women without jobs. Singer Bruce Springsteen insured his voice for $6 million! What would you insure?

Business Insurance

People need protection from the risk of accidents, disasters, and crime. So do businesses. In fact, insurance ranks as one of the most vital requirements for any business.

Why do businesses need insurance? Without proper insurance, a business can go from success to **bankruptcy** in the blink of an eye. Think about the different things that could happen to a business.

A business differs from a home in many ways. Businesses usually employ workers to provide a product or service. The number of employees can range from one or two people to hundreds or even thousands of people. Some businesses use dangerous and complicated machinery to make their product. They must properly train workers to operate it safely. Every business is responsible for the health and safety of its workers.

▼ Businesses have insurance to protect themselves against lawsuits.

Many businesses open their doors to customers. They must provide a safe environment for them, too. Businesses may sell their products to customers across the country or even across the world. These products have to be safely delivered. Furthermore, the product itself must be safe for people to use.

Kinds of Business Insurance

If a worker is hurt on the job, if a shipment goes missing, or a product causes harm to a customer, the business can be **sued** for damages. This can cost the business thousands or even millions of dollars.

With so many possible risks, proper insurance is vital for any business. **Property insurance** protects buildings and equipment. **Liability insurance** covers a business when it is sued for **negligence** or carelessness.

Many companies have business interruption insurance. Say a storm causes damage to a business because of flooding. Property insurance will help pay to repair the damages. Business interruption insurance can help cover the cost of lost production during the repairs.

Business owners pay their workers, but many pay an extra amount to the government for **unemployment insurance**. Many workers are entitled to receive financial assistance for a period of time if they lose their jobs. Business owners also pay an extra amount to the government for employee safety. This is commonly known as **workers' compensation**. Employees who are hurt on the job will receive financial assistance until they are able to work again. Most workers also pay a portion of their wages to cover the cost of this government insurance.

My House!
My Stuff!

Every summer, there are reports about forest fires and wildfires. For example, the state of California and the province of British Columbia suffered much damage from out-of-control fires during the summer of 2009.

◄ Wildfires destroy many houses each year.

People can't control the weather. Hot, dry weather, lightning, careless campfires, and even arson can cause a major disaster. These fires can destroy hundreds of homes and force thousands of people to evacuate. People can lose their homes and possessions.

Insurance can protect people when a disaster occurs, such as forest fires. Most people have insurance on their homes and possessions. Then, should disaster strike, they can rebuild their houses and replace their furniture, appliances, electronics, clothing, and other personal items.

To Insure or Not to Insure

Many people do not have insurance because they cannot afford it. Without insurance, they will not receive any money if their homes and property are damaged or destroyed. In the case of large-scale natural disasters such as hurricanes or earthquakes, the government may step in. It can provide some emergency funding to help victims resume their day-to-day lives.

Some people cannot purchase insurance for their homes, even if they want to. Insurance companies can refuse to provide coverage if a home is located in a high-risk area. This includes houses near rivers, lakes, or oceans that are under a threat of flood damage. It also includes many semi-arid regions subject to wildfires. These home owners often see the value of their property fall because they cannot get coverage.

Economics and YOU

Imagine that your family has just lost your home to a fire. Contact your insurance agent immediately. The agent will inspect the damage and provide a check within a few days to cover the cost of your temporary living expenses. As for the house itself, a good insurance policy will cover the cost of rebuilding your home.

▼ Homes must be rebuilt after wildfires.

What if I Get Sick?

The first kind of insurance that comes to most people's minds is medical insurance. Almost everyone needs medical care at some point in their life so medical insurance is very important.

Most of us become ill from time to time and require treatment or medication from a doctor. Health insurance helps pay for some or all of the cost of medical treatment.

Health Insurance Plans

There are many different kinds of health insurance. In some countries, such as Canada, the government provides health insurance for all legal residents. This type of insurance is commonly referred to as **Medicare**. People can see a doctor or stay in a hospital at no cost to themselves. The doctor or hospital sends the bill for their treatment to the government.

The advantage of Medicare is that it allows people to get the health care they need without worrying about its cost. Among its disadvantages are the added costs to the government which can cause taxes to go up. People may also have to wait longer for tests and treatment.

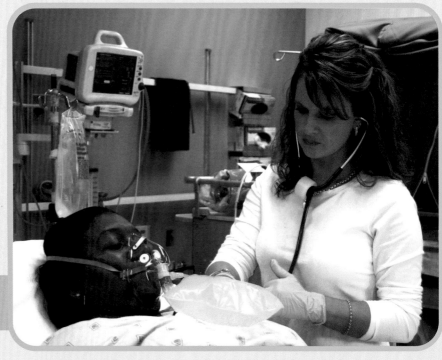

▶ Insurance helps people pay hospital bills.

◀ In Canada, health care is paid for by the government. People use hospitals like this one.

HMO and PPO

Many people have health insurance through an **HMO (Health Maintenance Organization)**. A number of businesses offer this type of health insurance to their employees as part of their **benefits** package. Employees may pay a small amount of their earnings in exchange for this coverage. However, they can only see doctors who are part of the HMO program.

Other people prefer to have a **PPO (Preferred Provider Organization)**. It is similar to an HMO, but people can consult with any doctor they choose, not just those who are part of the HMO. It costs people more to have this type of plan.

The cost of health insurance will vary from person to person. Overweight people or smokers will pay higher premiums. In some cases, they may even be refused health insurance.

Economics and YOU

What if you or someone in your family gets sick, but you cannot afford health insurance? In 1965, the United States established a program called **Medicaid**. It offers health insurance coverage to certain low-income individuals or families. The rules for qualifying are different from state to state.

What if I Lose My Job?

A major reason that people work is to pay their bills and support their families. Their future depends on their jobs. Unemployment insurance protects people from financial problems should they lose their jobs.

Let's say your mother works at a bank and your father works at a restaurant. Your family lives in a comfortable house. Suddenly, the economy slows down, and many people cannot repay their bank loans. The bank closes, and your mother loses her job. People in your city or town have very little extra money and stop eating at restaurants. Your father is laid off because the restaurant does not need as many employees. How will your parents pay all their bills?

Both your mother and father would receive unemployment insurance. This money would not be equal to their salaries. The payments would only be a portion of their earnings. However, the payments would provide some money to live on while your parents search for new jobs.

▼ People look for work at unemployment offices.

Different countries handle unemployment insurance in different ways. In the United States, each state maintains its own program. Each state also receives funding from the federal government to help pay for this insurance. Employers pay taxes to both federal and state governments to fund the program. In Canada, both employees and employers pay unemployment insurance. Premiums are based on the worker's earnings. These premiums are paid to an unemployment insurance fund. This fund pays for all unemployment claims instead of the government.

Not everyone can receive unemployment insurance when they lose their jobs. If workers are fired for poor performance, they will not qualify. Also, most workers must be employed for a minimum period of time before receiving unemployment insurance.

▲ Small business owners often get their insurance through local organizations.

Insurance for the Self-Employed

Many business owners or people who are **self-employed** do not qualify for unemployment insurance. In Canada, they do not have to use any of their income to pay into the insurance pool. If their business fails, though, they are not covered and so, are not eligible to receive any payments.

Some American states have recently offered a Self-Employment Assistance Program. It encourages those without jobs to start their own small business. They receive payments from the government while they are taking part in training programs and getting their businesses started. The payments equal what they would have received in unemployment insurance payments.

Point of Information

Local organizations, such as the Chamber of Commerce, often sell insurance to small business owners. The owners become a member of the organization and then they can purchase insurance for themselves and their workers from the organization.

What About the Future?

Most people like to plan for the future. They want their families to be safe and protected if anything should happen to them. One way to protect your family is to have **life insurance**.

Why do people buy life insurance? For several years, it helps replace the income that the deceased family member would have earned. For example, parents will often buy life insurance for themselves so their children are provided for if they should die.

Life insurance financially protects remaining family members. It helps to replace the income for several years that the deceased family member would have earned. Life insurance gives everyone in a family peace of mind.

▼ Insurance agents help people find the best policies for their needs.

Term and Whole Life Insurance

The most popular types of life insurance include **whole life insurance** and **term life insurance**. Term life insurance offers protection for a specific period of time. It might be 5, 10, or 20 years. The amount of your monthly premium never changes during the term. In case of death, your family would receive the face value of the policy. When the time period ends, the policy is worthless. However, you can renew the policy for an additional period of time. The cost of term insurance will increase when you renew a policy. That's because the older you get, the higher the risk of death.

Point of Information

The average annual cost of a life insurance policy is around $500. The rate varies depending on a person's age, job, family medical history, and whether or not they smoke. The greater the risk, the higher the cost of a policy. The policy cost also depends on its value. You will pay higher premiums for a million-dollar policy as opposed to a $200,000 policy.

Whole life insurance provides the same protection as a term life policy but it also includes an extra "savings" portion. The policy remains in force for your entire life. You will pay higher monthly premiums, but the policy will usually build some cash value. Whole life insurance serves as protection and also as a type of savings account. You can even borrow those savings in a time of need. Being able to borrow money provides extra protection to people in times of need and it is why people buy this kind of life insurance.

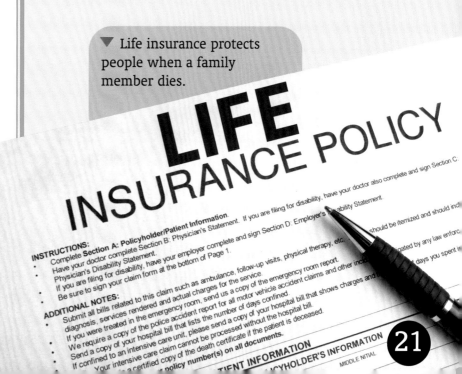

▼ Life insurance protects people when a family member dies.

Group Insurance

People and businesses need insurance for protection. So do different groups, such as governments, industries, and banks.

Governments of cities, towns, and municipalities need liability insurance. This protects the government against claims of damage or injury on public property or involving government employees. Someone's car can be damaged after hitting a large pothole on a city street. The city sewer system can back up and flood people's basements. A child may be hurt falling off playground equipment at the local park. In each of these cases, a government can be sued for damages.

Insurance for each community can be very expensive. Some communities have joined a group and together, they are able to purchase liability insurance at a cheaper rate. For example, many municipalities in the state of Michigan have formed the Michigan Municipal League. Through the League, liability insurance is affordable for each municipality.

▼ Towns keep their roads in good repair to avoid lawsuits.

Group Insurance

Group insurance helps protect the municipalities in Michigan. It also allows them to offer group health insurance to their employees, such as the police, firefighters, and administrators. By combining together, the municipalities get cheaper rates.

Industries also join forces with other businesses in their field to get affordable rates. Many individual businesses could not otherwise afford insurance to protect themselves or their employees. Some industries and individuals that join together for this purpose include farmers, logging companies and sawmills, trucking companies, small business owners, and self-employed people.

▼ This is President Franklin D. Roosevelt.

Economics in Action

During the 1930s, the United States experienced a severe economic **depression**. A depression is a time when business is very slow and many people are out of work. During this time, some banks closed. People lost all the money they had deposited in those banks.

In 1933, President Franklin D. Roosevelt signed the Banking Act of 1933. The act established the **Federal Deposit Insurance Corporation (FDIC)**. The FDIC insures bank deposits. Now people do not lose any insured funds if a bank fails. Currently, the FDIC insures bank deposits up to $250,000.

How Do I Get Insurance?

It's clear we all need insurance, but how do we get it? There are steps you need to take to get insurance.

Let's say you just bought a car. You need insurance before you can drive it. Start by choosing an insurance company. Insurance companies may specialize in only a certain kind of insurance. They might sell just automobile insurance or health insurance. So, locate several companies that sell automobile insurance, and then choose the one that offers the best coverage at the lowest price.

Your insurance company will ask a lot of questions and request that you fill out forms. This information helps the company decide how much to charge you for the insurance. The company uses **statistics**, or numbers and facts collected over time, to help it decide how much of a risk you are.

For example, history shows that young drivers have more automobile accidents. The risk of young drivers having an accident is greater than for other ages. That's the reason young drivers must pay more for automobile insurance.

▶ Teens who take driver education courses pay less for their car insurance.

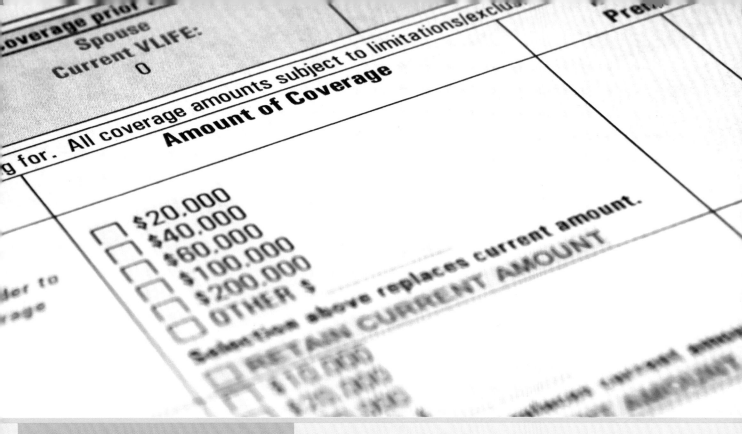

▲ It is important to make sure you have the right kind of insurance coverage.

Your Insurance Policy

The insurance company decides if you are a good risk. Sometimes, it turns you down but usually, it agrees to insure you. You receive an insurance policy, a contract between you and the insurance company. This policy explains what the insurance company has agreed to do.

The company asks you to pay a premium in exchange for the insurance. Once you pay the premium, the insurance company agrees to pay you if you have an accident. The payment may cover the cost of car repairs. You may be badly injured and can no longer work because you are confined to a wheelchair. The payments you receive could help you pay your costs of living so you do not lose your home.

Point of Information

On average, there are more than 6 million car accidents per year in the United States. Often when people have accidents, their premiums go up.

Insurance policies can be complicated. Like many other kinds of insurance, automobile insurance policies have to be renewed every year. You will want to compare policies from different companies to be sure you have picked the best one for you. The cost of the policy is just one thing to think about. Be sure to look carefully at exactly what the policy covers.

Shopping Around

You know all about shopping. Everyone wants to compare prices and find the best deal. Shopping for insurance is no different. You want to find an insurance policy at the best price.

Premiums

Many factors affect your premiums. You've already seen that your age affects the cost of automobile insurance. If you drive carefully for a few years, the cost will usually go down. Rates may also be lower if you complete a safe-driving course. You can even get a discount for good school grades. If you are listed as a "partial" driver on someone else's policy, your rates will be lower, too.

On the other hand, you may pay higher rates if you live in a large city, or if you drive an expensive car. This is because the risk is higher. More accidents take place in large cities. Fancy cars cost more to repair.

▼ It's important to drive carefully and avoid accidents.

The amount of your premium can also be affected by the amount of your **deductible** payment. The deductible is the amount of money you agree to pay for repairs or a replacement vehicle before you receive insurance money. If you agree to pay for the first $500 in damage, you will pay a certain premium. If you agree to pay the first $1,000, your premiums will be lower.

Comparing Companies

It is important to check the reputation of the insurance company you wish to use. Cheap isn't always better! Some companies honor a policy and pay quickly. Other companies challenge every claim or take a long time to pay. Ask plenty of questions. Check with friends and family members for advice.

Insurance Brokers

Different companies will charge a range of prices. So, it pays to investigate. You may choose to deal with an insurance **broker**. An insurance agent represents only one insurance company, while a broker represents the insurance buyer and can deal with many companies.

▼ Insurance brokers can help you find the best deal.

▼ Sports cars cost more to insure. Can you guess why?

27

Is Insurance Ever Bad?

We all need insurance, but how much do we need? Do we need it for everything? When should we buy insurance and when should we say no?

Sometimes, people buy insurance when it is not needed. There may be little risk, or you may already be covered under another policy. For example, your family decides to buy a new microwave oven. It already comes with a **warranty** from the company that built it. A warranty guarantees that if the product doesn't work it will be repaired at no extra cost. The microwave oven warranty lasts two years, but the store offers to sell you an **extended warranty**. It promises to repair the oven if it breaks within two years after the original warranty ends.

Sounds good, right? However, most people never use the extended warranty. There is little risk of the oven breaking so soon after the original warranty expires. The cost of the extended warranty may be about the same as the cost of a new microwave. So consider how much you are paying for insurance and if it is really necessary.

▼ Extended warranties on small appliances are not often worthwhile.

Point of Information

During the holiday season of 2007, consumers in the United States paid an estimated $1 billion for extended warranties on electronics and appliances.

Insurance and You

We all need insurance because it protects our families and our businesses. Not having any insurance would be the same as a tightrope walker at the circus not using a safety net. One mistake and that performer could be in big trouble.

No one wants to have an accident, lose a job, get sick, or suffer a natural disaster. Many of us must face this reality, though. When it does happen, an insurance policy can be of tremendous help. The money from your claim can help buy a new car or home if they are damaged or destroyed.

Insurance can help pay your bills until you find another job. It can help pay for medicine or treatment if you get sick. Insurance allows all of us to work together to help those who are in need. Insurance also gives us peace of mind. We feel better because we know if something happens to us, our families, our neighbors, or our co-workers, insurance will provide protection and help.

Glossary

bankruptcy When an individual or a business cannot pay what is owed

benefits Payments made to workers in the form of health, unemployment, or other kinds of insurance; employees may pay a small amount of their earnings in exchange

broker Someone who represents the insurance buyer and can deal with many companies to get the best price

claim Request for payment based on an insurance policy as the result of loss

coverage The extent to which an insurance policy offers protection

damages Harm or injury to a person or property

deductible The amount of money someone agrees to pay for repairs or a replacement before that person receives insurance money

depression A time when business is very slow and many people are out of work

extended warranty A form of insurance that covers damage to something for one or two years after the original warranty ends

Federal Deposit Insurance Corporation (FDIC) Government agency that insures bank deposits

HMO (Health Maintenance Organization) A group of health professionals who provide medical support to enrolled members and their families

insurance Financial protection against loss or damage

invest To use money to buy something that will make more money

levee An embankment built along a body of water to keep the water from overflowing onto land

liability insurance Insurance that protects a business when it is sued for negligence; if the business loses the case, its insurance pays the fine

life insurance Insurance that provides a cash payment to family members if someone dies

Medicaid Health insurance for certain low-income individuals or families; rules for qualifying are different from state to state

Medicare A type of government-provided insurance in which people can see a doctor or stay in a hospital at no cost to themselves

negligence Carelessness

policy A contract between an individual or a business and an insurance company listing the obligations of each party

PPO (Preferred Provider Organization) Health insurance that is similar to an HMO but people can consult with any doctor they choose, not just those who are part of the HMO; participants pay more to have this type of plan

premium The fee paid for insurance coverage

profit The amount of money left after all the costs of running a business have been paid

property insurance Insurance that protects buildings and equipment and pays for whatever is lost in a fire or other disaster

risk Chance of loss or harm

self-employed Someone who works for themselves and not as an employee of a business or organization

statistics Numbers and facts collected over time

sue To start a case against someone in a court of law

term life insurance Protection for a specific period of time, with the amount of the monthly premium never changing; in case of death, the insured's family members receive the face value of the policy; if the insured has not died by the end of the time period, the policy is worthless

unemployment insurance Financial assistance given for a limited period of time to workers who have lost their jobs

warranty An insurance policy that guarantees a product will work for a limited period of time or the product will be repaired at no extra cost

whole life insurance Protection that remains in force for the insured's entire life; higher monthly premiums than for term insurance but the policy will usually build cash value

workers' compensation Financial assistance given to employees who are hurt on the job until they are able to work again

Index

Webfinder

www.hc-sc.gc.ca/hcs-sss/medi-assur/index-eng.php
www.investopedia.com/features/insurance-101.aspx
www.nchc.org/
www.iii.org/